AF585268

AUSTRALIAN LANDSCAPES

WATER

IN AUSTRALIA

RACHEL DIXON

REDBACK publishing

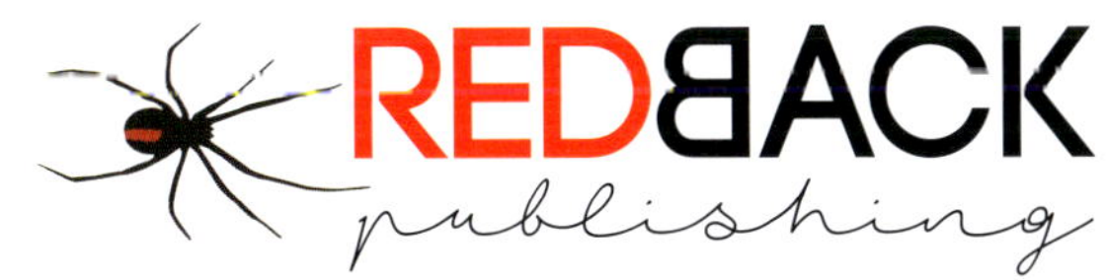

First published 2018 by
Redback Publishing
PO Box 357 Frenchs Forest NSW 2086
Australia

ISBN 978-1-925630-23-7

Author: Rachel Dixon
Editor: Jane Hinchey
Original illustrations © Redback Publishing 2018
Originated by Redback Publishing
Printed and bound in China by Leo Paper

MIX
Paper from responsible sources
FSC® C020056

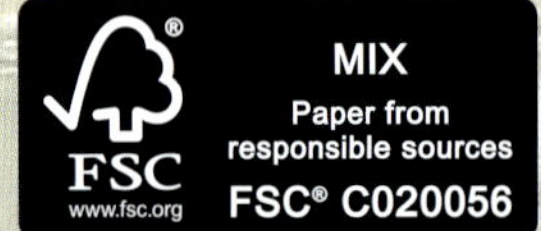

Acknowledgements:
Abbreviations: l—left, r—right, b—bottom, t—top, c—centre, m—middle
We would like to thank the following for permission to reproduce photographs: p4b - state library nsw, p6t, p14t - State Library of Victoria, p7t - National Gallery of Victoria, (p22t - Martyma, p24t - Bidgee, p28b - Przemys¤aw JahrAutorem, p29t - Hiltonj, p31b - ZooPro all via Wikimedia)

Cataloguing-in-Publication details are available from the National Library of Australia

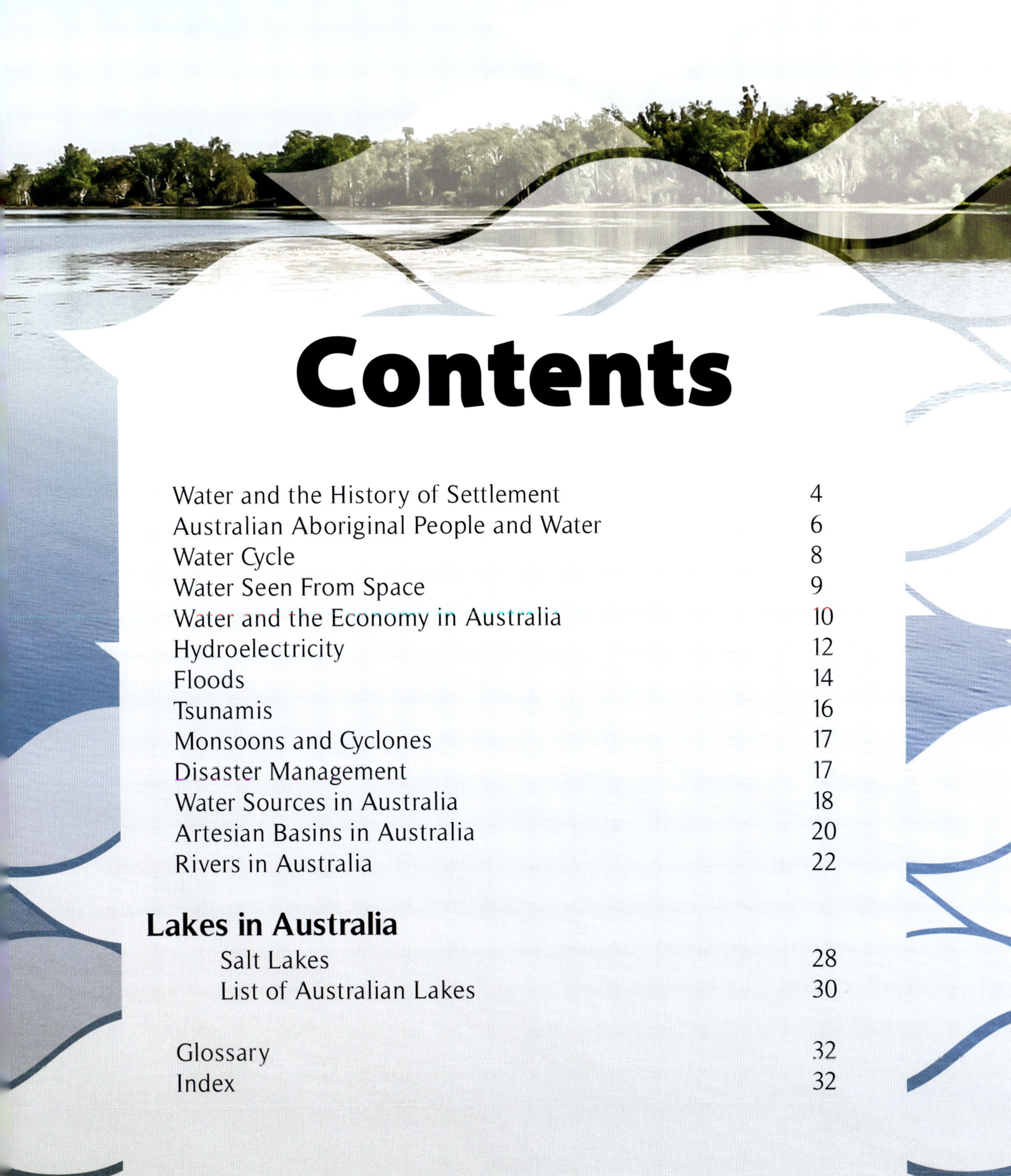

Contents

Australia is the second driest continent on Earth, after the Antarctic. Water has defined the spread of human settlement, from the arrival of the first Aboriginal Australians over 60,000 years ago, right up until the present. Seen from space, the lights of Australia's cities show how the population is concentrated around the coasts and in regions supplied with a reliable water supply.

Water is precious in Australia and it is not a free resource. Householders, businesses and farmers all pay to use water and there are many regulations controlling how it is taken and the disposal of wastewater.

Water and the History of Settlement

The lack of fresh water on the northwestern part of the Australian coast was one of the reasons Dutch explorers of the 17th century decided the land was of little value for colonisation.

When Governor Phillip arrived from Britain with the First Fleet in 1788, he found that Botany Bay did not have a supply of fresh water, so he had to find somewhere else to land. The spot he chose in Sydney Harbour was on the banks of the Tank Stream.

In the following years, the state capital cities of Sydney, Hobart, Perth, Brisbane, Melbourne and Adelaide were all founded near rivers or streams. The location of the water sources determined where people settled and how towns could expand.

Early explorers rowed boats up rivers and creeks to discover what lay beyond settlements, travelling much further than they would have been able to on land. In 1830, Charles Sturt became the first explorer to reach the southern coast by rowing a boat all the way along the Murray River to its mouth at the ocean.

Apart from providing a water source, rivers were needed for transport. It took years before roads and railways were built. In the meantime, settlers travelled on boats using waterways. Miners and farmers sent their ore and agricultural produce to towns for sale using river transport on barges, paddle steamers and sailing ships. These methods of transport were quicker and safer than using the poorly maintained tracks on land, and violent encounters with bushrangers were avoided.

Above left: Old Tank Stream Sydney, 1852 Right top: Murray River today

Murray
Lachlan
Adelaide
Murrumbidgee
Sydney
Murray
Melbourne
STURT'S JOURNEY

Australian Aboriginal People and Water

Rainbow Serpent

Many Dreaming stories from Aboriginal nations refer to serpents that created rivers. These Rainbow Serpents have many names. The twisting shapes of the riverbeds were formed as the serpents moved across the land during the Dreamtime.

Food

The waterways of Australia offered Aboriginal people sources of plant and animal wildlife for food. Fish and eel traps using stone walls were built on creeks and rivers. Canoes made from bark or logs were used for transport and for fishing. Sometimes a fire would be built on the canoe so that a meal could be cooked without having to go back to land.

Water in Deserts

In the deserts, the location of water sources was knowledge that was committed to memory by Elders and shared using ceremonies and artwork. Some of the dot paintings that are prized by art collectors around the world are based on water maps.

Although the deserts are dry on the surface, many of them have groundwater that comes to the surface as springs. Remembering where these springs were located was a matter of life or death for Aboriginal people. They also actively dug and maintained wells. In 1906, when Europeans were surveying the Canning Stock Route across the desert in Western Australia, they relied on local Aboriginal people to tell them where the water sources were. Concerned at the destruction of the precious springs and wells, some Aboriginal people refused to disclose this information and were treated violently as a result.

Land and Water Rights

Traditional Aboriginal land ownership involves ownership of the water flowing through it as well. Land rights determinations do not automatically give traditional owners the right to take water from rivers. They also cannot alter waterways, such as by building small dams to collect fish. Aboriginal Land Councils usually have to apply separately for a cultural water licence to make use of water sources.

Above: Serpent Dreaming, Aboriginal painting   Below: The Bunyip

Billabongs

A billabong is a lake that is left behind when a river changes course, usually after a flood has receded. The wildlife in large billabongs can include crocodiles, fish and water birds, but small billabongs may simply dry up and disappear. Billabongs feature in Australian Aboriginal cultural stories as places of spiritual importance. A legendary monster called the bunyip is supposed to live in billabongs.

Water Cycle

Water is the only compound (H2O) that exists naturally on Earth in the three states of matter, as a solid, liquid and gas. Water moves through all these states of matter in a process called the Water Cycle.

1. Liquid water on the Earth's surface evaporates into water vapour in the atmosphere.
2. Water vapour cools and falls as rain, ice or snow.
3. Liquid water runs into rivers that empty into oceans or it seeps underground.
4. Liquid water on the surface evaporates and starts the cycle over again.

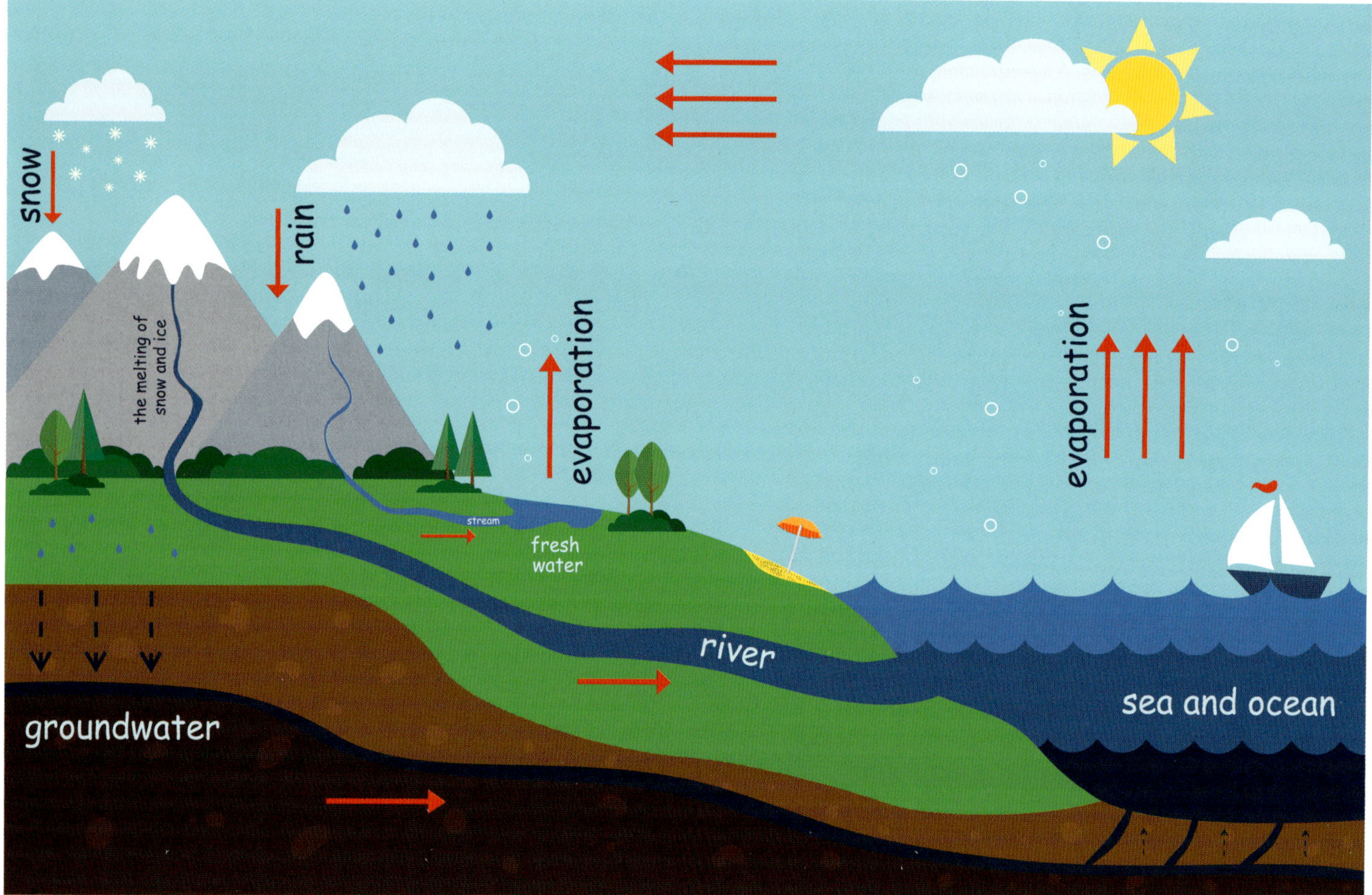

- In Australia's deserts and savannahs, the water that runs into rivers may never reach the ocean, as it evaporates too quickly.
- Groundwater does not evaporate until it comes to the surface as springs or through bores made by people. It may also seep into rivers or the ocean.
- Trees contribute to the water vapour in the atmosphere by drawing water up and releasing it through their leaves. This is called transpiration.

Because of the Water Cycle, all water on earth is interconnected. Overuse or pollution of a water resource in one location does not destroy the water, but does make it unusable by living things in that place

Water seen from Space

Geoscience Australia has compiled an online resource with Landsat satellite images of the water sources across the country. Australia's main centres of population and farming are located where the concentration of water sources is highest.

Across Western Australia, the cattle industry depends on the large grassed savannahs. Although the water sources there are not as numerous as they are in the eastern states, the satellite images show that there are large areas of water in the savannah regions.

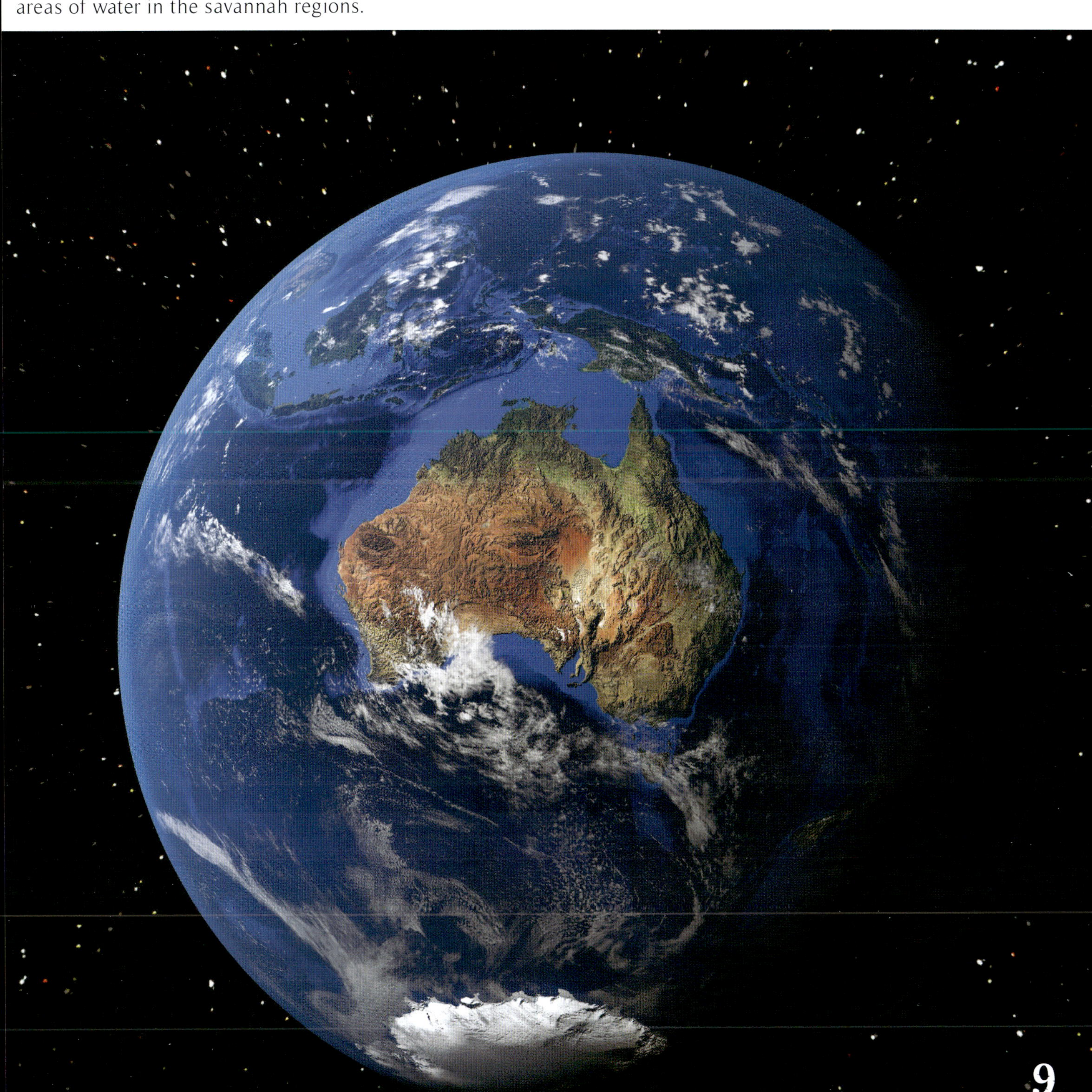

Water and the Economy in Australia

Business activity in Australia is concentrated in areas with reliable and plentiful water supplies. There are more jobs available in these areas and the economic productivity of well-watered areas is higher than in arid regions.

Agriculture

Farmers need water to grow crops. The cheapest source of water for them is rainfall since they do not have to pay for it. If farmers only use irrigation, they have to buy the water and the cost of growing their produce is higher, which means consumers have to pay more for it in shops.

Livestock

Different types of livestock businesses require differing amounts of water to operate. Dairy farming needs large amounts of water, both to grow lush pastures and to operate the farming equipment, so these types of businesses are not usually set up in semi-arid regions. Cattle farmers can run large herds in the semi-arid savannahs using only bore water.

Mining

Many types of mining require large amounts of water to operate. If there is no water available, either the mine cannot be established, or water has to be brought from other areas. This increases the cost of production and reduces the profitability of the mine as a business.

Tourism

Tourism in Australia depends on rivers, lakes and other waterways being in a condition that is attractive for tourists. Along the Murray River, low water levels can affect the number of tourists choosing to go there for their holidays.

Real Estate

The release of land for building new houses depends on a water supply being available. Large parts of Australia cannot be developed for housing because there is not sufficient water to supply any new residents.

The National Water Initiative sets the guidelines for governments around Australia to manage their water resources. Factors they consider are:

- the environment
- who has the right to use water resources
- pricing for water storage and delivery
- the management of water for towns and cities

Hydroelectricity

Hydroelectricity is a renewable resource. It is generated when water falls on the turbines in a power station. The spinning turbines lead to the creation of electricity. There are about 100 hydroelectric plants in Australia. They are located in areas of high rainfall and high altitude. There is little scope for expansion of hydroelectricity technology in Australia due to the lack of further water sources that could be used. Most of the sources that are suitable have already been developed. The large areas of flat land in the interior of Australia are a barrier to the expansion of hydroelectric schemes, because the water source needs to be high enough to give the falling water power to drive the turbines.

Hydroelectricity generators operate in New South Wales, Tasmania, Victoria, Western Australia, Queensland and South Australia.

The Snowy Mountains Hydro-electric Scheme in New South Wales is the largest hydroelectricity operation in Australia. It was completed in 1974 and comprises a number of dams and generators. Water from the Snowy, Eucumbene and Murrumbidgee Rivers is diverted and used to produce electricity. It is then released into the Murray River and the Murrumbidgee River, where it is used for agriculture and to maintain the water levels in those rivers.

The Snowy Scheme is one of the most impressive civil engineering projects ever undertaken anywhere worldwide. Sixteen dams, 145 kilometres of tunnels, hundreds of kilometres of piping, a pumping station and nine power stations were constructed between 1949 and 1974. More than 100,000 people came from over thirty countries to work on the project.

Below: Water pipes to the powerstation in the Snowy Mountains

Floods

Early Settlers

Building houses and farms near rivers made the first settlers vulnerable when floods occurred. The flooding that destroyed so many colonial lives and farms was much more severe after colonisation than it had been before. Unlike the Aboriginal people before them, early settlers cleared land, allowing topsoil to enter rivers. This silted them up and contributed to damaging floods spreading across the treeless land. In New South Wales in 1810, Governor Macquarie founded the town of Windsor on the Hawkesbury River to provide a place of refuge for local farmers when the river flooded. He gave orders for the building of four more towns for the same reason, and for the township of Liverpool on the Georges River, which had also burst its banks in flood.

Above: Settlers clearing land

Flood Mitigation

In modern suburbs, where most of the land is covered with buildings, concrete and bitumen, rain cannot soak into the soil and enters stormwater drains instead These often empty into creeks and rivers that cannot hold the extra water during high rainfall, resulting in flooding. Governments in some of these flood-prone areas have introduced building regulations that make landowners store their stormwater in specially constructed pits. This rainwater is then released slowly to reduce the risk of flooding.

Above: Raging flood waters in Central outback Australia

Causes of flooding

- poor land clearing practices
- unusually high rainfall
- tsunamis
- storm surges causing the sea to flood onto the land
- dam failure upstream from the point of flooding
- having large, flat areas of land near a flooded river or stream, as in inland Australia
- blocked drainage systems in built-up areas

Floods in Deserts

Although deserts are normally dry, sandy places, sudden flash flooding can occur and dry creeks can suddenly become dangerous. Campers should never set up their tents in a dry creek bed, even if there is no sign of rain. In Australia's deserts, the monsoon rain that falls in the north flows down watercourses and results in more southerly dry riverbeds quickly turning into flowing rivers. Water may also spread out to form swamplands. Coopers Creek and the Diamantina River are two examples of waterways that go through these cycles of dryness and flood, a common pattern for rivers through desert and savannah regions of Australia.

Tsunamis

A tsunami is a large wave of water that travels long distances. They are produced by an earthquake or landslide on the ocean floor. When the wave reaches land it flows over the coast and causes flooding.

Tsunamis occur around the Australian coast but their effect has been much less damaging than in countries such as Indonesia or Japan. The highest tsunami on the east coast was measured at one metre high at Sydney in 1960. This was the result of an earthquake in Chile, in South America. The northwestern coast of Australia is more vulnerable to tsunamis because of its exposure to waves coming from earthquakes in Indonesia. Tsunami waves along this part of the Australian coast have included the following:

- **1977** - six metre tsunami wave recorded at Cape Leveque, WA
- **1994** - four metre tsunami wave travelled 300 metres inland at Exmouth, WA
- **2006** - tsunami wave forced water 200 metres inland at Steep Point, WA

The Joint Australian Tsunami Warning Centre monitors tsunamis and warns Australians if there is a possible threat to coastal communities.

Monsoons and Cyclones

The northern part of Australia has a monsoonal climate. There are only two main seasons annually, the wet season and the dry season. During the wet season, heavy rainfall fills empty creeks and rivers that had dried up during the dry season.

Cyclones are a natural weather event in northern Australia. Mangrove forests help to stabilise the coastline and reduce damage by cyclones, but many mangroves have been removed to provide building sites and harbour structures. The most destructive cyclone in modern times was Cyclone Tracy in Darwin. It occurred on Christmas Day 1974, flattening whole areas of Darwin. Many people died or were injured as a result of the cyclone.

Disaster Management

Disaster management in Australia is coordinated by government organisations, but every person experiencing a natural disaster can play a role as well. In extreme emergency situations, the Australian Defence Force may be asked to assist. Floods, cyclones, tsunamis and storm surges are all natural disaster events that need a disaster management plan. The four steps in such a plan are:

- prevention
- preparedness
- response
- recovery

Once a hazard, such as flooding, has been identified, government bodies then assess the risk to the community by looking at:

- How high the flood will be
- The buildings, farms, bridges and other structures that will be affected
- The number of people who will be affected

Above: Cyclone Marcia 2015 Morayfield Below: Cyclone Debbie 2017 Queensland

Water Sources in Australia

A permanent source of water is vital for any human settlement. The first settlers in Australia used rivers, creeks, wells and rainwater. Many attempts at farming had to be abandoned when settlers found that water was not always available at the location they had chosen for their farm.

Rivers and Creeks

In the early days of settlement, water drawn from rivers and creeks was unpolluted, unless the source was near a dead animal or had been contaminated by humans nearby. Parasites in river water have always been present. As populations grew, rivers were used as both a source of drinking water and a place to dispose of sewage and other waste. Today, towns that draw their water from rivers need to filter and purify it.

Water in Semi-Arid Areas

The only permanent water source in Australia's semi-arid areas comes from groundwater. This is either pumped to the surface through bores or it occurs naturally as springs. Bore water is used to feed livestock, for mining operations and for household needs. Farm dams are impractical in the arid regions of Australia as the evaporation rate is so high.

On the edge of deserts, such as at Eucla, sand hindered any attempts to build towns. The Eucla Telegraph Station was once one of the most important communication centres in the region but it is now a ruin and half buried in sand. The lack of water meant that plants could not survive and there were no root systems to hold the sandy soil in place.

Dams

As populations grew, rivers were dammed to provide the reliable water sources people and businesses needed. A dam is much more than just the structure that holds back the river water. The whole area that provides the runoff for that river needs to be managed so that chemicals, dead animals or sewage do not pollute water entering the system. Tributaries of the main river also need to be controlled.

In 1972, the Ord River Dam and Lake Argyle provided water for agriculture in the Kimberley region in Western Australia. Lake Argyle is also a local centre for water sports, swimming and recreational fishing. The nearby town of Kununurra was built as the service centre for the irrigation project, which includes both the Ord River Dam and the Kununurra Dam.

Warragamba Dam was built in 1960. It is Sydney's main water source and the largest dam for urban water supply in Australia. Its extensive catchment is the Burragorang State Conservation Area.

Carting Water

By the 1820s, the first settlement at Sydney had polluted the Tank Stream and water had to be carted in from nearby swamps to supply the people's needs. In many rural areas around Australia, householders still get some or all of their water from tanker deliveries.

Below: Warragamba Dam

Rainwater Tanks

Rainwater for household and garden use is usually collected from the roofs of buildings. Rainwater tanks were once only common in rural areas, but recent droughts, and a concern for sustainability, have encouraged city dwellers to install tanks in their yards as well. People who use these tanks for drinking water need to be sure that runoff from the roof does not contain dangerous chemicals or lead from paint.

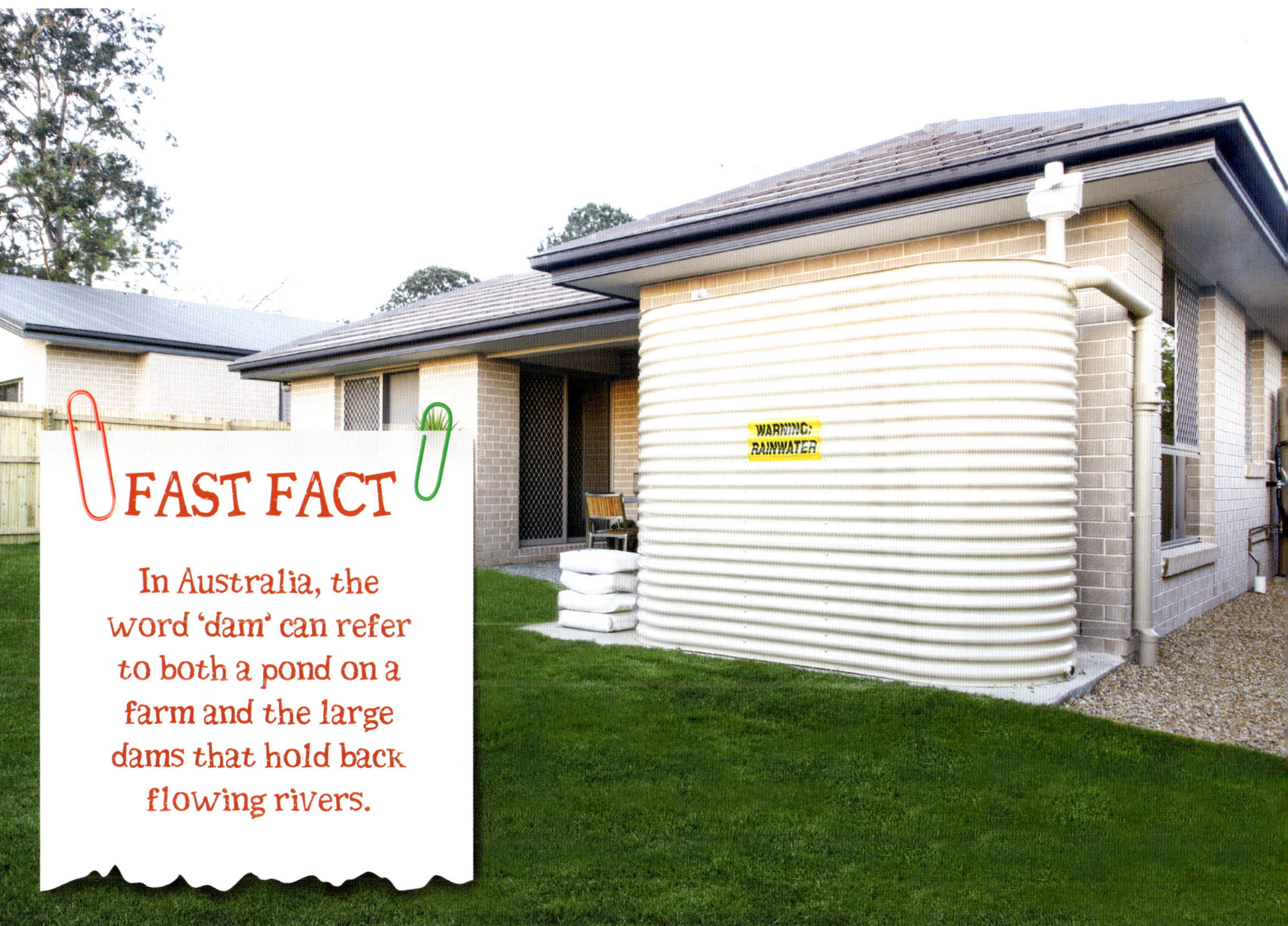

Desalination Plants

Seawater cannot be used for drinking, washing or cleaning because of its high salt content. Salt water is corrosive and will destroy metal in pipes and in objects such as cars. Desalination plants remove the salt from seawater, producing freshwater. Western Australia has two desalination plants, and the states of Queensland, New South Wales, South Australia and Victoria each have one.

Recycled Water

Water recycled from wastewater, such as sewage and stormwater runoff is not used widely in Australia. Some private households recycle their own water but there are building regulations in cities that control how this can be done. In particular, the reuse of sewage water requires strict controls on the design of piping and storage to avoid the spread of disease. In all states and territories, recycled water is available in some areas for irrigation but not directly for drinking. In New South Wales, recycled water is released into the Hawkesbury Nepean River to keep the flow at a high level. In Western Australia, treated wastewater is returned to underground natural aquifers, from where it can be pumped out for reuse.

Artesian Basins in Australia

Australia is well-supplied with many artesian water basins or natural underground water sources. Most of this water is millions of years old, although some basins receive topups from surface water seeping into them. The Great Artesian Basin lies beneath large areas of New South Wales, Queensland and South Australia, spreading across one fifth of Australia. Other large groundwater sources are the Murray Darling Basin, the Perth Basin, the Canning Basin, the Daly Basin and the Otway Basin. These basins, along with the many smaller ones, supply Australia with an extensive water resource, although much of it is too salty for drinking or agriculture.

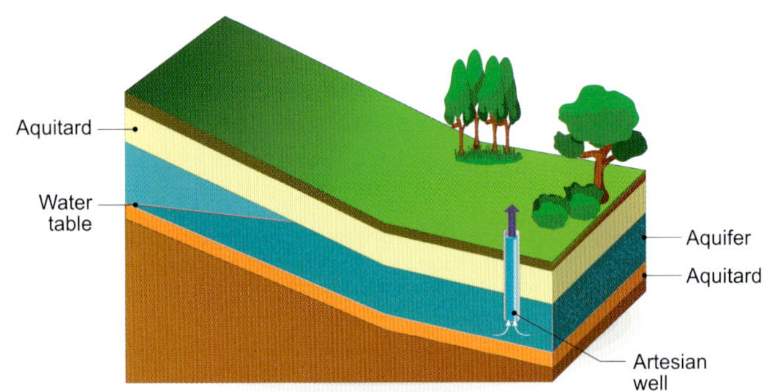

Artesian water either flows naturally to the surface in springs, or it is pumped to the surface. Over time, mineral deposits in the water can cause a mound to build up around a natural spring. These mound springs were very important for the traditional Aboriginal lifestyle, wildlife and livestock. Water from the mound flows around it creating a pool, which can be a permanent oasis in the desert. The Witjira-Dalhousie Springs is an area of over 50,000 hectares that contains 60 springs. It is a National Heritage listed site.

Below: Windmill pumping water from bore

Soil Salinity and Groundwater

Soil salinity occurs when poor agricultural practices lead to a rise in the underground water level. This brings salty water up near the surface, causing the destruction of plant life. The salt also makes bore water unsuitable for drinking by humans or animals. Farmers can reduce soil salinity by keeping the ground covered in plants that have deep root systems, and by not allowing large areas of land to remain bare of plants.

Sustainability of Groundwater Sources

Overuse of groundwater leads to the depletion of a resource, which was created millions of years ago. The flow pressure can be reduced across the whole system through overuse in one location. Increasing population and the strength of the cattle and mining industries have all caused extra bore water to be drawn from groundwater basins across Australia. Pumping too much groundwater can lead to the drying up of natural springs fed from the same source.

Surface Environment and Groundwater

Mound springs form isolated oases in the desert. Animals that live in or around these springs either die or have to move across arid lands to other habitats if the mound spring dries up.

Above: Hot artesian bore outback Queensland

Coal Seam Gas Mining

In Queensland, coal seam gas extraction involves the removal of very large quantities of groundwater and affects the Great Artesian Basin. Fracking is the fracturing of coal beds to release the gas. This fracturing can lead to contamination of groundwater sources that are used for drinking and agriculture.

Rivers in Australia

Murray Darling River System

Location

The water that enters The Murray Darling Basin is drained from an area that covers about 14 per cent of Australia. This huge river system is half the length of the Nile River in Africa. The source of the Darling River is in Queensland. It joins the Murray River, which then flows through New South Wales towards the sea and the South Australian coast.

Description

The Murray Darling System has thousands of creeks as its tributaries. Under the surface there is groundwater that is fed by seepage from the rivers. Water in the rivers is taken in large amounts for agriculture and, when combined with periods of drought, this can cause the water level to fall. Governments have had to control inflows to the rivers from the Snowy Mountains Scheme and also regulate the amount farmers can draw with the aim of restoring the Murray River to its former higher flow.

People

The Murray Darling Basin supports two million people, their agriculture and industries. The varied habitats for native plants and animals range from alpine to semi-arid along the course of the rivers. The Murray River is a tourist attraction and government bodies controlling the release of water from dams upstream attempt to ensure that water levels in the river are high enough for any special water events that are being held. Businesses that have invested in houseboats and paddle steamers that operate on the Murray River need to have high water levels in the river to attract tourists.

Wildlife

The river red gums that have evolved to grow on the swampy flood plain are iconic symbols of the Murray River. They cannot survive if the river level falls and their surroundings become too dry. The Native Fish Strategy aims to increase the fish in the Murray Darling System back to 60 per cent of the numbers before settlement occurred.

New South Wales Rivers

Murrumbidgee River

The Murrumbidgee River flows through New South Wales and the Australian Capital Territory. Its source is in the Australian Alps. The Murrumbidgee River is the third longest river in Australia and it is a tributary of the Murray River. The large town of Wagga Wagga is located on a floodplain on the banks of the Murrumbidgee River, so the town has been subjected to many floods.

The Wiradjuri people are the traditional inhabitants of the Murrumbidgee River area. They form the largest Aboriginal nation in New South Wales. The Murrumbidgee Irrigation Area was created in 1903. It still provides water for farmers who produce a large proportion of the agricultural produce from New South Wales.

Above: Murrumbidgee River

Parramatta River

The Parramatta River is important to the history of Australia. The first inland exploration by settlers in 1788 was undertaken in a boat rowed up the Parramatta River from Sydney Cove. The Parramatta River flows into Sydney Harbour.

Northern Territory Rivers

Above: Finke River

Finke River

The Finke River is one of the most ancient river systems in the world. It runs through the Finke Gorge, the area that inspired Aboriginal artist, Albert Namatjira. During the dry season, parts of the riverbed are dry and are used as a road by travellers. In the wet season, the Finke River is subject to flooding.

Victoria River

The Victoria River rises near the Judbarra / Gregory National Park and enters the sea on the northern coast of Australia. Although there are crocodiles living in the river, boating and fishing are popular with tourists to the region.

Queensland Rivers

Cooper Creek

Explorers Burke and Wills camped beside Cooper Creek in 1860. They died tragically in the desert soon after returning from their trek to the north of Australia. Cooper Creek, and its tributaries the Thomson River and Barcoo River, go through an annual cycle of drying out and flooding. Their water empties into Kati Thanda - Lake Eyre in South Australia.

Flinders River

The longest river in Queensland, the Flinders River rises in the north of the state and enters the sea at the Gulf of Carpentaria. It flows through the Porcupine Gorge National Park. Land beside the Flinders River supports cattle and agriculture, and dams provide water for irrigation.

Diamantina River

The Diamantina River rises in central Queensland and empties into Kati Thanda - Lake Eyre. When it is in flood, the Diamantina River has a poorly defined course, as its waters spread a long distance out across the flat land. During the dry season, water in the river may not flow any further south than the Goyder Lagoon, which is about 250 kilometres away from Kati Thanda - Lake Eyre.

Below: Cooper Creek

South Australian Rivers

River Torrens

Adelaide was founded on the banks of the River Torrens, and the upper parts of the river still supply Adelaide with water. In the 1830s, the river alternated between flooding and being a series of waterholes.

Murray River

The Murray River enters the sea near Goolwa in South Australia. It also flows into the Coorong Wetlands that include 140 kilometres of lagoon, freshwater lakes, the river mouth and ocean beaches.

Tasmanian Rivers

Derwent River

The Derwent River has its source in Lake St Clair and it flows into the sea through a large harbour that was one of the reasons for the founding of Hobart. Hydroelectric power stations operate on the Derwent River's tributaries upstream.

Franklin River

The Franklin River was at the centre of a large conservation movement in the 1980s. Protesters opposed the damming of the Franklin River because of the damage this would cause to World Heritage listed wilderness. It took a High Court ruling to finally stop work on the Franklin dam.

South Esk River

The South Esk River is the longest river in Tasmania. It joins the Tamar River at Launceston and flows into the sea at Bass Strait.

Below: The Derwent River

Victorian Rivers

Goulburn River

The Goulburn River is the longest river in Victoria and is an important water source for agriculture along its course. It rises in the Victorian Alps and joins the Murray River. The Goulburn River in Victoria should not be confused with the Goulburn River in New South Wales.

Yarra River

Melbourne was founded on the banks of the Yarra River, which flows into the sea at Port Phillip. Today, the Yarra River contributes to Melbourne's character. Its riverside parks and waters are popular recreation spots for the city's residents.

Above: Yarra River

Western Australian Rivers

Swan River

The Swan River reaches the sea at Fremantle. One of the reasons Perth was founded on this site was that the mouth of the river provided a good harbour. Settlers wanting to travel further inland initially used boats on the river for transport rather than trying to find a way through the bush.

Great Dividing Range

This mountain range runs along most of eastern Australia. Rivers that have their source in this range either flow east towards the Pacific Ocean or inland.

Above: Ord River

Ord River

The Ord River in the East Kimberley region of Western Australia is the site of the Ord River Irrigation Scheme. Lake Argyle was created as part of this scheme, and is the largest artificial lake in the southern hemisphere. The damming of the Ord River captures its wet season flows and makes them available for agriculture all year round. Before it was dammed, the Ord River was reduced to a series of waterholes during the dry season.

Gascoyne River

The Gascoyne River is the longest river in Western Australia. It only flows for part of the year. When it is dry, farmers and residents living along its course draw water from the groundwater basins that exist beneath the dry riverbed. The Gascoyne River enters the Indian Ocean at Carnarvon, where the surrounding desert meets the sea.

Lakes in Australia

Salt Lakes

Many of Australia's rivers empty into salt lakes. Monsoonal rainfall in the north of Australia sends water along rivers and creeks that are often either completely empty during the dry season, or have been reduced to a series of unconnected waterholes. The sudden flooding of these rivers can surprise travellers, since the water can start flowing even though there has been no rain in the local area.

How Salt Lakes Form

The flooding of these dry rivers can lead to a sheet of water spreading across the flat landscape in desert regions. These temporary wetlands form vast lakes that attract migratory birds. As the wetland evaporates, a series of waterholes is left. Finally, after all the water is gone, only the salt is left behind. This is how the salt lakes are formed.

Australian Aboriginal People and Salt Lakes

Salt lakes in the deserts are included in the Dreaming stories and song cycles of the Aboriginal people who are the traditional custodians of that area. Some salt lakes are the homes of dangerous spirit creatures, while ancestor spirits created others as they journeyed through the country.

Salt Lakes and Sport

The flat surface of salt lakes makes them a destination for people who race cars for sport and others who enjoy land yacht sailing. Lake Gairdner in South Australia is the venue for a large sporting gathering where all types of motor vehicles race each other across the dry salt surface. Donald Campbell set a land speed world record on Lake Eyre in 1964 in his racing car Bluebird. He travelled at 648.7 km/h.

Below: Lake Gairdner Inset: Donald Campbell's Bluebird

Kati Thanda - Lake Eyre

The best known and largest salt lake in Australia is Kati Thanda - Lake Eyre in South Australia. It is 700 kilometres north of Adelaide and is the lowest point in Australia, at about 15 metres below sea level. As the lake fills, thousands of waterbirds migrate to it. They include birds that are normally only seen in seaside locations, such as pelicans, gulls and terns. The birds feed on insects and on the small fish that multiply in the lake. The wetland extends for 144 kilometres but it is only temporary. When the water evaporates, animals and plants die and migratory birds leave. The drought resistant eggs of fish and insects, as well as plant seeds, have all been left in the lake as it dries, waiting for the next flow of water before they start to grow.

Above: Kati Thanda - Lake Eyre

Salt Lakes in Australia

Lake Amadeus, NT
Lake Ballard, WA
Kati Thanda - Lake Eyre, SA
Lake Frome, SA
Lake Torrens, SA
Lake Lefroy, WA
Lake Gairdner, SA
Pink Lake (Hutt Lagoon), WA
Pink Lakes, VIC

List of Australian Lakes

Gippsland Lakes, VIC - lakes and wetlands that are a popular tourist destination
Great Lake, TAS - the original small lake was enlarged when the Miena Dam was built
Lake Argyle, WA - created as part of the Ord River Irrigation Scheme
Lake Burley Griffin, ACT - an artificial lake in Canberra
Lake Colac, VIC - a salty inland lake that completely dries during drought
Lake Cootharaba, QLD - in the Great Sandy National Park
Lake Corangamite, VIC - Australia's largest permanent lake, although in times of drought its waters become saltier than seawater
Lake Dalrymple, QLD - formed when the Burdekin River was dammed in 1987
Lake Eucumbene, NSW - created when the Eucumbene River was dammed as part of the Snowy Mountains Scheme
Lake Gordon, TAS - a lake created when a dam was built on the upper reaches of the Gordon River
Lake Hillier, WA - a pink lake on Middle Island
Lake Mackay, WA - cycles between dryness and filling with flood water
Lake Macquarie, NSW - the largest coastal lagoon in Australia
Lake Pedder, TAS - the subject of protests by conservationists who opposed the flooding of Lake Pedder when the Gordon River was dammed
Lake St Clair, TAS - Australia's deepest lake and the source of the Derwent River
Myall Lakes, NSW - a rare example of natural ecosystems and their interactions, largely unspoiled by human interference
Willandra Lakes, NSW - a World Heritage Site

Ramsar Convention

This is an international treaty that provides guidelines for the conservation of wetlands around the world. Most of the United Nations countries, including Australia, have agreed to follow these guidelines. There are 65 Ramsar Sites in Australia that have been listed as Wetlands of International Importance.

Below: Lake Pedder, Tasmania

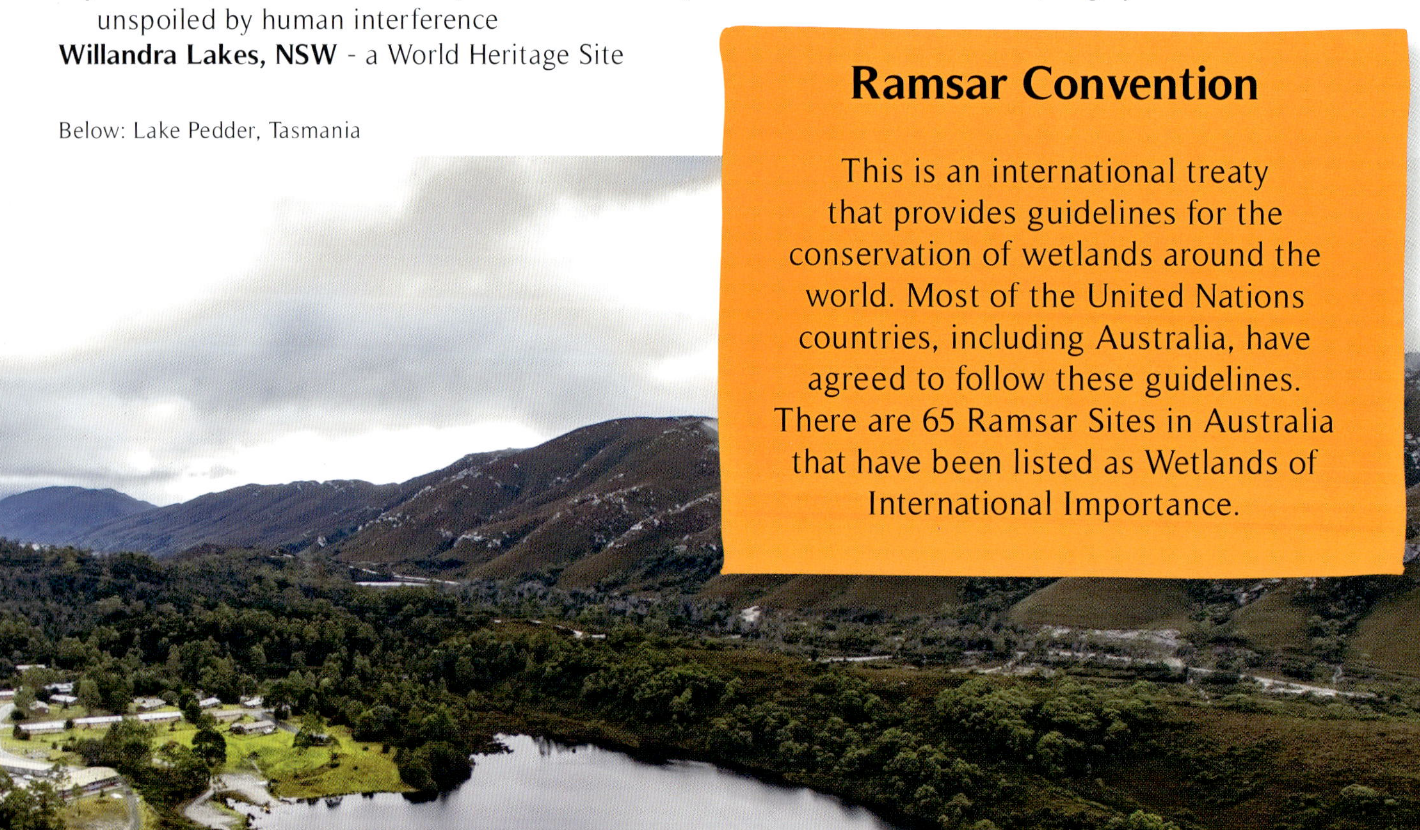

Australia's Two Amphibious Mammals

An amphibious mammal is able to live on both land and water.

Australia has two of these unique creatures.

Platypus

The platypus is a monotreme mammal that lays eggs. It has a duck-like bill and flattened tail. Scientists first thought that the dead specimens they were given to examine were not real. They could not believe that such an animal could really exist. The platypus hunts underwater and builds a burrow that can only be reached through an underwater entrance.

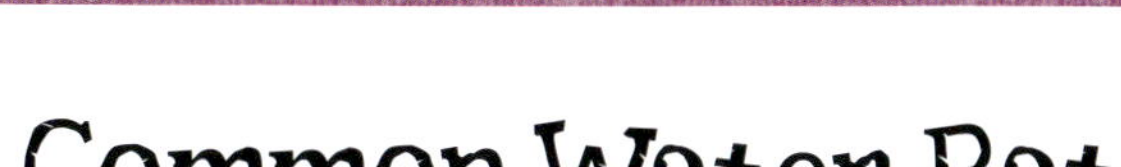

Common Water Rat

The water rat is a placental mammal, meaning that it gives birth to live babies. It has water resistant fur and webbed feet, allowing it to hunt underwater. It can be identified by the white tip on its tail.

Glossary

alpine area	elevated area above which trees cannot grow
aquifer	rocks underground that store water
groundwater	underground water in rocks or soil
lagoon	saltwater lake beside the ocean
migratory animals	animals which regularly travel to different regions
mitigate	reduce or lessen something
oasis	spring in a desert
savannah	grassland landscape with only a few trees and bushes
turbine	revolving machine

Index

Visit these websites to find out more about Water in Australia:
www.agriculture.gov.au
www.bom.gov.au/water